# The Time is NOW

## The Ultimate Guide to Becoming Physically, Spiritually, & Financially Free

Terence Young, ACB

Published – November 2017

Copyright © 2017 by Terence E. Young

**The Time Is Always NOW – The Ultimate Guide to Becoming Physically, Spiritually & Financially Free**

**ISBN - 9781978437654**

Connect with TY

www.terenceyoungnow.com

Facebook: Terence Young – New Thought Transformational Speaker

Twitter: @tyoung1122

Instagram: @terenceyoungnow

Printed in the United States of America

All rights reserved under International Copyright Law. This book or any portion thereof may not be reproduced or used in any manner whatsoever without the express written permission of the writer.

# *Table of Contents*

Acknowledgements 4

Introduction 6

Chapter 1 - That ain't the way I see it! 8

Chapter 2 - Love is my religion 28

Chapter 3 - Do you understand the words that are coming out of my mouth? 44

Chapter 4 - Do I really have to jump? 59

Chapter 5 - Control what you can control 72

Chapter 6 - Yesterday you said tomorrow 84

References 99

# Acknowledgements

This book has been a labor of love for me over the past year and although I am the author I certainly didn't do it by myself. I couldn't have written this book without the support of my family and friends.

To my wife Amy Kieper Young. Thank you for your unconditional love and understanding as I spent many late nights writing and/or editing to get this project complete. I recognize the sacrifice that it took on your part and I am truly grateful.

To my Children, Terence Young and Yaniece Young. Thank you for helping me become a better man and a better father every day. It has been a blessing to watch you grow into the responsible young adults that you are. I am so proud of both of you.

To my Mother and Father, Peggy Young and Willie Fred Young, Sr. Thank you for the many life lessons you taught me throughout the years. I know I would never have developed into the man I am today without your guidance and love.

To my brothers, Michael, Will, and Chris Young. You guys already know! It's been a journey for all of us. Thank you for being an inspiration to me.

To Michael, Mark and Matthew. I am blessed to have you in my life NOW. Thank you for keeping me on point and reminding me what it's like to be a kid again.

To Rev. Virginia Walsh & the Unity North Tampa family. Thank you for guiding me to my purpose on this planet. I am forever grateful to you and our wonderful Spiritual Community at Unity North Tampa.

To my editor Vicki Procinski. Thank you for your tireless efforts to make this book project the best that it can be.

And last, but not least, to my pets; Ally, Cinnamon and Sugar. Thank you for teaching me a level of patience I didn't know I had... :)

I love you all. Let's get it in...

# Introduction

Have you been procrastinating on starting a new chapter of your life because you feel like it's not the right time? Are you one of those people that say "I will get around to it" and never get around to it? Are you dealing with an addiction that is affecting your life negatively, but you don't know how to overcome it? Has fear been holding you back from living your life to its fullest potential? If you answered yes to any of these questions then this book is for you. By reading "The Time is Always NOW - The Ultimate Guide to becoming Physically, Spiritually and Financially Free" you will learn how to conquer fear by uncovering the truth of where it stems from. You will learn the 3 most important steps of time management to help organize your days and utilize your precious time more wisely and most importantly you will discover how to remove any negative thoughts or self-defeating behaviors from your life in an instant by harnessing the power in the eternal moment of NOW.

Self-sabotage is a real thing. I wrote this book to help people who want to make a change in their lives, but can't seem to get out of their own way. I wrote this book to help people who want to escape the shell of their own excuses and live life illimitable! I know how it feels to be buried by your fears and indecisive on what the next move should be for your life. I've been there too, so this book is as much for me as it is for you. I stumbled upon a power that has changed my life forever and NOW I have written this book to share that awareness with you.

I designed each chapter with stories to illustrate the 6 Key Attributes that make up this life guide. They are

- Perspective
- Love
- Communication
- Overcoming Fear
- Time Management
- NOW

Each chapter includes stories to illustrate the 6 Key Attributes. Each chapter also includes sections entitled "Physically/Spiritually/Financially". These sections illustrate how each attribute can be used to influence this specific part of your life. At the end of each chapter, I have a "What Can I Do NOW?" section. This section has exercises that you do right NOW to put these principles into action. I encourage you to complete the exercises and read the suggested books to get the most out of this guide.

The great teacher, Dr. Michael Bernard Beckwith, once said "Stories shouldn't begin with 'once upon time'; they should begin with 'once upon a choice'." Life is all about our choices. Today is the beginning of your new story. What choices will you make? Let's begin! What are your waiting for? The Time is Always NOW...

# Chapter I - "That ain't the way I see it!"

*"When you change the way you look at things, the things you look at change" - Dr. Wayne Dyer*

That quote from Wayne is one of the best quotes ever said. It holds so much truth in it. It speaks to the truth about perspective and how all of life is not what happens but how you react to what happens. Picture if you will:

Two men work for the same company as outside sales reps. First guy wakes up looks outside. Pouring down rain! He says to himself. Today is going to be a terrible day to make sales because all the decision makers will be out of the office because of this terrible weather. I might as well stay home.

Second guy wakes up, looks outside. Pouring down rain! He says to himself. Today is going to be a great day to make sales because all the decision makers will be in their office because of this weather. I can't wait to get started and close sales today.

Let's analyze this scenario for a minute. The two men have the exact same outside circumstances; same city, same weather, same job. So, what's different? The way they choose to see them. What's on the inside is what's different. These two men have a very different perspective on the way this day is going to go. Who do you think had the better day?

You guessed it. Sales guy number two had the better day. Why? Because he expected it to be a great day, it was.

Our lives are completely controlled by our perspective of the world. Most people have a limited perspective of the world and what they are capable of doing with their lives.

When your perspective is limited, your life is limited. One of my favorite quotes is "We don't see the world as it is, we see the world as we are."

A perfect example would be the political climate in the United States at this present moment. Never has there been a time when we were more polarized than we are right now. It's simple; we have two different parties who fundamentally see the world two different ways. In addition, these two parties also see the solution to fixing America's problems very differently. As I write this, Donald J. Trump is the President of the United States of America. He just put into place an Executive order issuing a ban on travel to the United States for citizens of 7 countries in the world. These countries are predominantly Muslim. Mr. Trump and his staff's reasoning for this ban is to protect America from "Radical Islamic Terrorism."

Now, the irony with this Executive order is that none of the terrorists that have attacked America in the past are from any of the countries on the list. The countries on the list are Iran, Iraq, Libya, Somalia, Syria, Sudan and Yemen. The 9/11 attackers were from Saudi Arabia, United Arab Emirates, and Lebanon. If President Trump was really concerned about protecting Americans from foreign terrorists, than wouldn't it make sense to have these countries on the list as well? Well, of course, it would, but that's not why this ban is in place. This ban was put into place because of Trump's perspective on the situation. What President Trump sees is a terrorist when he sees someone who practices the Muslim faith. Since this is the way he sees it, his policies are reflecting his perception of the situation. Of course, this couldn't be further from the truth because the vast majority of Muslims are peaceful, loving people who want the same things for their family as we want for ours; *peace, love, joy, harmony, faith, justice*. Just to be fair to President Trump, he's not the only one who sees it his way. Millions of Americans actually agree with him, and, of course, millions of American's don't…

What's most important to understand, though, is this, whether you agree with President Trump or not: the perspective of the leader of the most powerful country in the world certainly makes a huge impact on the entire world. We are watching it unfold first-hand.

The beautiful thing about perspective is it can change and we are totally in control of our perspective. I pray this will happen to bring peace to our world.

## What do you believe?

Let's bring it closer to home. Not about the world, or your country, or your city, how about you? What is your perspective? Not about Trump. Let's get off politics. What is your perspective about life... about your life? About where you can go, what you can achieve??

While preparing for this book I read "The I of The Storm" by Gary Simmons. It was an amazing read. One of the passages that truly struck me was this:

*"All conflicts possess an element of misperception. When we stop and consider the mechanics of perception, we can readily appreciate the enormous effort it takes to truly understand another person. Our capacity to accurately read a situation is influenced by how we see things, how we hear what's being said, and how okay we feel about ourselves..." (The I of the Storm - Gary Simmons)*

As the passage states, we must take the time to realize the enormous effort it takes to truly see things from a different perspective. In other words, we have to be able to see things from the other person's point of view. I love the illustration of the two people looking at a number from opposite sides. One says it's a 6, the other says it's a 9. Both are telling the other that they are "wrong." Turns out neither one of them are wrong. They are both right, they are just seeing the same thing from a different perspective. We must learn how to take the time to walk a mile in another person's shoes before we make a rash judgement about them.

The beautiful thing about this is it is natural for us to have different perspectives. I find it ironic that so many people have a difficult time when someone disagrees with them. Of course, they disagreed with you! They are not you and they have a totally different perspective on the situation than you do. Has it ever dawned on you that you are unique in every way? No one in the world is exactly like you. On the grand scale, yes, we are more alike than we are different (we're all human beings, we all want the same things...etc...) however we are also very different in a myriad of ways. Of course, there are the obvious things that are different about us such as we are males and females, different ethnic backgrounds, and such. But some of the things we don't think about that make a huge difference in our perspective on the world are:

1) Age
2) Religion
3) Environment

Let's take a look at these in detail...

*Age* - Ever watch a small child at play?? Everything's a miracle. And, oh man, the questions! It's pretty obvious to us as parents that our children have a different perspective on life than we do. We expect that. We have the greatest idea, and buy the most awesome gift ever for Christmas, and we think they are going to love playing with it all the time. And, they would rather play with the box that it came in. Perspective ...

I have great conversations with my adult children now. Yes, they are adults now, Terence is 21 and Yaniece is 18. They are my best teachers because every time they do something that I don't approve of I have to go back and review my perspective of the world when I was their age... It's tough, but most of the time I recognize that TY at age 21 probably was doing most of the things that Lil T is doing now. So, how can I judge him for doing something that I did? Now that's not to say I don't give him advice so he doesn't have to make the same mistakes that I made. I just stop at the point of judging him for making mistakes. Sometimes that is exactly what people need. It reminds me of a powerful truth... God doesn't make mistakes... It is happening and unfolding exactly how it should.

I have great conversations with my Mother. But, we have a totally different perspective on the world and rightfully so. She grew up in the 50's and 60's. I grew up in the 70's and 80's. We, literally, grew up in two different worlds. When she was a child, there were Black bathrooms and White bathrooms. Black water fountains and White water fountains. I've only read about that stuff in books and seen it in the movies. I've never lived in a world like that, but she did. This, of course, affects our perspective on the world as a whole. And, yes, we disagree on topics all the time, but it's ok because that's the way it should be. Remember this the next time you are talking with your parents or someone from a different generation than yours. Your perspectives on everything can be totally different because they grew up in a different world than you. The important thing to remember is they are not against you. No one is against you because we are all part of the one body of Christ.

***Religion*** - Religion can have a drastic effect on how someone sees the world. Take this illustration for example.

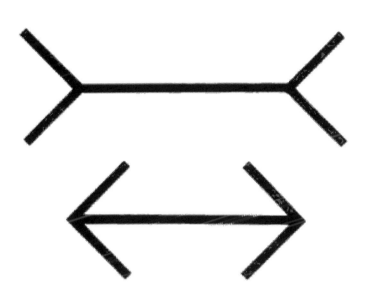

Which line is longer? Some of you may have guessed the top one, but you would be wrong. The answer is they are both the same length. Recent studies have shown that Americans and Europeans are more readily fooled by this illusion than other groups of people. Why is that? The fact is there is a connection between religion and worldview.

Cultural diversities are vast throughout the world and this type of phenomenon is particularly attributed to whether a person sees the BIG picture or the little things. NOW, I'm not going to say that all people in a certain religion are this way or that way, however what I am saying is there is a correlation. People who grow up practicing the religions of the East such as Hinduism, Buddhism, Jainism, Sikhism, Taoism, Shinto and Confucianism all tend to be more apt to see the big picture. In other words, they can see the forest and the trees. People who grow up practicing the religions of the West such as Judaism, Christianity and Islam, tend to be more apt to seeing the little things, but might miss the big picture. In other words, they can't see the forest for the trees.

Having said that, even within Christianity, there are differences. Let's look at this. Traditional Christianity preaches to a God in Heaven, separate from us. In Unity (which considers itself to be practical Christianity), we speak from a God that is within us. There is a difference. And that difference can affect the way we see the world. If you are dealing with a financial shortage and your rent is late. If you believe that God is up there in Heaven you would feel this way about it...

*"Why is this happening to me God?? I keep doing all the right things yet I'm still behind on my rent. I just don't understand... Dear God can you pleeeeease help me? My rent is due and all I'm asking is that*

*you send some money down here or send someone to bring me some money down here so I can pay my rent. Amen...*

Now, on the contrary, if you believe that God is within you and you are dealing with the same financial shortage, you would look at it totally differently and would feel this way about it.

*"Thank you, God, for giving me this opportunity to grow. I know that all things are working for my good in divine order so I welcome the opportunity to learn the lesson within the valley that I'm traveling through right now. Thank you, God. In the name and in the nature of the Christ and so it is..."*

Both people are dealing with the same scenario, but their perspectives are drastically different. This is the power of religion on perspective.

**Environment -** Can your perspective on life be different based on your environment? Of course, it can. If you live in certain areas of Chicago you wake up every day dealing with a city in turmoil. As I write this book, I'm reading through an article that states that Chicago, the nation's third largest city, had 762 murders in 2016. It was the deadliest year in 2 decades. (CNN article By Amanda Wills, Sergio Hernandez and Marlena Baldacci, CNN Jan. 1st 2017).

If you lived on the Southside of Chicago in 2016, your perspective on life might sound something like this...

*"The world is such a dangerous place. I just pray that I can get to work safe and my kids can be safe at school. Why is there so much violence in the world?"*

In comparison if you were living in Melbourne Australia in 2016, where the homicide rate is extremely low (3.1 per 100,000 Wikipedia), your perspective on life might sound like this.

*"I really love my life and the city I live in, mate. Every day I wake up excited to see what new adventure I can take on. Now, let's grab a vegemite sandwich and be on our way!"*

Two different cities; two totally different perspectives. Of course, you don't have to be on the other side of the word to experience this. I could have just as easily used San Francisco (which is one of the Unites States' safest cities) in the above scenario, but minus the "Mate" and "Vegemite sandwich."

The question is can these variables affect your perspective? Yes. Do they have to affect it? NO! I started this chapter with this quote "When you change the way you look at things, the things you look at change."

Let's analyze that quote. "When **YOU** change the way **YOU** look at things, the things **YOU** look at change." Let me ask you a question. What's changing? You or the "things?" The answer is YOU.

You are changing and that is the key to using your perspective to become Physically, Spiritually and Financially free.

## *Physically - Spiritually - Financially*

If you are feeling **Physically** ill you can call it a disease or you can call it a blessing from God. My mother recently went to the doctor for a check-up and to get some medication because she had been battling what she thought was a bad cold. Once the doctor saw her, she called the ambulance and sent my mom straight to the hospital where she was diagnosed with pneumonia. My mother spent a week in the hospital before being released. NOW there are two ways to look at this;

1) What a burden it was for my Mom to spend that week in the hospital. The food was terrible. She was uncomfortable. What's that ambulance bill gonna be! etc... or
2) What a blessing that she went to the doctor that day. The fact that she went to the doctor, and the doctor was able to see how sick she was, and that she needed immediate medical attention in the hospital may have saved her life.

How do you choose to see your physical ailments? There is freedom in gaining the perspective of how they have blessed you. Do it and watch how it changes your life for the better.

If you are lacking **Spiritual** guidance, focus on your perspective. I pray for my children all the time. The truth is, though, you can't really pray *for* someone. You can only pray *with* someone. There comes a time in life where you must let people go, so they can fly on their own. It's tough as a parent, but it is also very true. Now, I'm not saying I don't offer up those prayers every night and twice on weekends for my two adult children. (You parents of adult children know what I'm talking about.) What I'm saying is there is freedom in letting go and knowing that they have all that they need. There is a beautiful song that I love to sing and part of the verse is "Where the spirit of the Lord is, there is freedom." Well the spirit of the Lord is in each and every one of us, so when we trust in that, there is no need to fear. God's got us!

If you are dealing with **Financial** stress, start by focusing on your perspective. Did you grow up in a house where you heard the phrase "money don't grow on trees" often? I did. This is the kind of predisposition to money that many people have. That statement is an affirmation of lack. We all know that, if you are feeling the vibration of lack, you will find a way to experience it in your life. Remember, you don't get what you want. You get what you are... If you are experiencing discomfort in your finances, than you probably have a misguided perspective on money.

Here's a question for you: If you are walking down the street and you drop $1 million dollars into a homeless person's cup, is he or she NOW a millionaire? Sadly, no is the answer. He or she is just a homeless person with a million dollars that will very soon go back to being homeless. Why? Because he has not gained the perspective on how to handle that money. This is why we have lottery winners, sports stars, and musicians who make millions of dollars. Then we see them on TV and they say they are broke. How could this be? Simple. The more money you make, the more money you spend. Here's a good rule of thumb. If you can't manage $30,000 a year, you can't manage $30,000,000 a year. No matter which amount you make, you will spend it all and go broke.

Here's the key, it's not about how much money you make. It's how much money you keep and how long you keep it for. In order to break this cycle, one must change the way he or she looks at money. Money isn't real it's just paper (Literally nowadays, but we won't get into that discussion here). What's real are the things that money can give us like Freedom. We must learn to save, invest and grow our money to become free of worry and financial stress. Find a good financial advisor that you trust. Spend some time learning how to save and invest for your and your family's future. You'll be glad you did.

## *Change your Perspective Change Your Life*

One of the first steps to becoming Physically, Spiritually and Financially free is to be cognizant of your perspective on life. It doesn't matter what's happening, it's how you choose to see it. There's what happens and there is the meaning you decide to give it. This is the key to mastering your perspective. Remember, when you change the way you look at things the things you look at change...

# *What Can I Do NOW?*

**I - Changing Perspectives** - Practice going back and forth between the different variations of what you see. Can you see both pictures?? This is an exercise on consciously changing your perspective.

Duck or Rabbit?

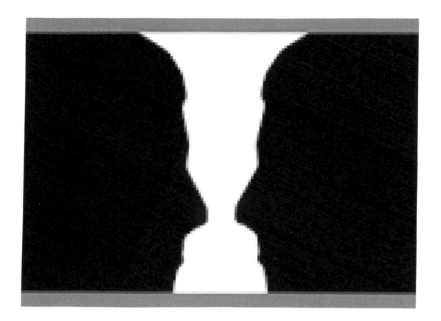

Faces or vase?

Columns or People?

Wife or Mother in Law?

## II - *The Belief Challenge*

1) Analyze your major beliefs about: life, family, work, play, politics, religion etc.

2) Take a piece of paper and write down "I believe... and fill in your answers about the above topics.

3) Take a second sheet of paper and write down "I believe"... and this time write the opposite of what you previously put down as your core beliefs. (Resist the urge to justify why you believe something, just write down the opposite or opposing answer. For example, you can use Democrat /Republican, Seminoles / Gators, College Education/ No College, Entrepreneur/Employee, Religion/No religion.

5) Here's the fun part. Go back and justify why you believe each one of them *on both sides*. For example, justify why you believe it's better to be a Democrat and then justify why it's better to be a Republican. Do this for all of your core beliefs. I know it's not easy, but have fun with it. Look for the good and you will find it.

If you haven't realized it yet, this is an exercise on perspective. Seeing things from the other person's point of view. Challenge your beliefs and you will start to see how we are a lot more alike than we are different.

# Chapter II - Love is my religion

*"Where there is love there is no darkness" - Burundian Proverb*

Summer 2008... I find myself sitting in the huge sanctuary of First Unity of St. Petersburg. This place was buzzing. Bustling with people of all walks of life, all ethnic backgrounds, and all religions. Yes, that's right "all religions." The sanctuary is shaped like a dome set off in a shaded area surrounded by 100 year old oak trees. There must have been 300-400 of the happiest people I've ever met in that building that day. They were all so nice which made me start thinking "What's wrong with these people?" This was my first experience attending a Unity Service. My girlfriend at the time had brought me to "her church." You see, by this time I had been a member of Water's Edge Church in Wesley Chapel for five years where I served on the music team and as the Children's Minister. Two weeks before we had gone to "my church" and, since I was on the music team and the Children's Minister, she got a chance to see what I did and how our service was. I can't remember exactly what the sermon was on that day, but what I do remember was her reaction afterwards. I remember asking her "Well, how did you like the service?" She responded "Well, I felt like it was kinda negative and nothing like my church and our service." This, of course, led into a major disagreement about what was so different about her church from my church. I didn't see any issue with what we were teaching and what I was teaching since I was the Children's Minister.

*We are all sinners and we are intrinsically bad. Jesus died on the cross for our sins and that gives us salvation. We must accept Jesus as our Lord and Savior and follow the teachings of Christianity, solely, or we are going straight to hell when we die. We could never be or do the things that Jesus did. Jesus was special. We need to repent of our sins, watch out for the devil and one day, Jesus is coming back to save us all. So... we... just... wait...*

*Right?*

I'm not attempting to sum up traditional Christianity in a few sentences but that is the gist of it.

Now, keep in mind I had been teaching traditional Christianity for years, including to my then two young children, Terence and Yaniece, so I felt pretty strongly about these teachings. Still, I agreed, begrudgingly, to attend a Unity service to see what all the fuss was about. I mean, she seemed so happy and her daughter seemed really happy with the Youth program. It couldn't be that bad, right? At least, that's the way I was feeling at the time.

# A Paradigm Shift

*Paradigm Shift: an important change that happens when the usual way of thinking about or doing something is replaced by a new and different way.*

Whoa!! Did you just read that? I mean did you really get it? When you experience a paradigm shift, your entire mind, body and spirit change in an instant. It's an amazing thing. This is what happened to me when I visited First Unity in St. Petersburg. I don't remember what the sermon was about, but I do know that Rev. Temple Hayes was speaking that day and that I found her to be extraordinary. She was confident, powerful, peaceful, positive, passionate and inspiring. When I left that day, I knew that there was something different about this "church service." Of course, NOW I know we in Unity like to call our Sunday services Spiritual gatherings or Spiritual Centers. Anyway, I couldn't quite put my finger on it but I just felt better about myself and my relationship with/to God when I left this place. The difference was palpable. I could feel it in every vein of my body. I left there a different man. Even though I continued on teaching at Water's Edge for another year or so it just wasn't the same. I didn't have the same unwavering belief in what I was teaching anymore. NOW I questioned some of those teachings. Things just never were the same for me after that. I still didn't quite know why.

# **Rock Bottom**

Fast forward to Summer 2009. I had just lost my job; well basically I stopped showing up for work so they let me go. I moved out of my one bedroom apartment because I couldn't pay the rent anymore and moved back in with my mother. *All of this was compounded by the fact that I had been abusing alcohol for, at least, the last 20 years. I was what some would call a functioning alcoholic. I would get up and go to work (for the most part) everyday, but the problem was I would drink every day, as well. It wasn't a good look and, eventually, led to me being in the situation that I was in.* As I was laying on the bed in the back bedroom, the same bedroom that I had grown up in as a kid, I heard this faint sound that just got louder and louder and louder - beep, beep, Beep Beep, BEEP, BEEP!! I heard my Mother call my name from the front porch. "Terry, Terry!!" Yes, she calls me Terry although I really don't like it. It's always stuck. My brothers also still call me Terry to this day. What can I say? Some things you just gotta live with. So, when I heard her I jumped up to see what was going on. As I got out to the front porch, I saw the tow truck driver hooking my Nissan Xterra up to the tow truck. Yeah, I couldn't make that payment, either. So, I went from having a nice three bedroom apartment, new car, and good job to no home, no car and no job. This was the beginning of the end for me. Of course, beginnings are always disguised as painful endings.

# **Revelation**

As expected, living with your Mother at 37 years old did not work out well. The whole "I'm an adult so don't tell me what to do" scenario played itself out several times before I decided it was time to go. Needless to say, I spent about 3-4 months there. My new beginning was starting as I began to pull myself out of this hole I had dug for myself. First I found a job. I hated the job, but at least I had one and I was grateful for that. Then, I found myself a great little one bedroom apartment in Temple Terrace. So, I moved. I had no furniture though. Thank God for my Mother because she gave me a bed to use and that was a huge blessing. My bigger issue though was I had no transportation. The commute took me two hours and three buses each way. I would catch the bus at 6:15am to get to work at 9am. Then, after work, catch another bus at 5:30pm and get home at 8pm. Did I mention I hated that job already? Well, just in case I forgot to mention it, I hated that job! I was a debt collector and I was terrible at it. All I kept thinking, as I was calling these people, was they were just like me and, if a debt collector called me, I would tell them I didn't have the money, too, and I wouldn't be lying! Needless to say, I wasn't a very good debt collector. I stayed there as long as I could, though, until something better came along. Those bus rides though were something else. It was there where I started to find myself. I would spend hours reading on the way into work and hours reading on the way back home. What was I reading? I started reading everything I could find on Spirituality. I knew that I wanted a deeper connection with the Christ that lives within me. I found myself reading Lao Tzu, Eckhart Tolle, Deepak Chopra, Wayne Dyer, Neale Donald Walsch, just to name a few. It was truly a revelation for me. This is where my Spirituality practice began. On the bus...

**January 2010** - By this time I had left my previous church and I was looking for a new Spiritual Community. I went to the internet to search. What was the first thing that came to mind? Unity. I searched for Unity Churches in the area. Very quickly, I found Unity North Tampa. I just so happened to have been reading Wayne Dyer's book, Excuses Begone, and had just finished The Power of NOW by Eckhart Tolle. When I looked at their website one of the first things I read was "If you like the teachings of Wayne Dyer and Eckhart Tolle you are going to love it here." I felt like "Wow! This has got to be the place for me!" Of course, the next question was how am I going to get there? Low and behold, there is a bus stop right in front of the building. It was like it was meant to be. I knew then that spirit was leading me to this place.

So, I visited to see what it was like. When I walked through the doors I remember thinking "Man, this just feels right." The room was fairly small but the love in this place was plenty! You enter through a small foyer and over to your left was the alter. Diagonally to the right I saw the keyboard player getting ready for the day's music. The place was lively and I was immediately greeted with a smiling face welcoming me that morning. This was so familiar because, again, meeting these people for the first time, I thought to myself these are some of the nicest and happiest people I have ever met. On my first visit, the minister was not there, they had a guest speaker, but I liked it so much that I decided to come back the next week to meet the minister. The following week I met Rev. Virginia Walsh. Rev, as I like to call her, is slim, tall, blonde, extremely confident, and extremely calm. She is a clear, confident, peaceful, passionate, loving speaker who embodies everything that Unity is. When Rev speaks, people listen. After meeting with Rev, I knew this was where God had directed me to be.

I attended Unity North Tampa regularly for a few years and remained very active in the congregation, especially working with the music team. I joined UNT as an official member in 2012.

I'll never forget that meeting with Rev. Virginia and a few other new members. We did a very powerful exercise. She asked us to write down the names of people that we admired. I wrote down a few names such as my mother, Mike Dooley, Martin Luther King Jr, Les Brown, and Jim Rohn. She, then, asked us to write down what it is about these people that we admire. I wrote down that they were compassionate, loving, outgoing, passionate speakers/people. I've always admired great speakers and I mean more than just "like" them.

I always studied them and wondered how they became that way. It's always intrigued me, but I never knew why. This was the day that I got my answer. Rev. looked over at all of us and, with that cool and calming voice, she said "the attributes that you admire in others are the attributes that you have within yourselves." That was the answer to my question! I knew that day that God had blessed me with ability to move people with my spoken words. I had found my passion.

None of this would have been possible had it not been for the truth I found in Unity. Being a part of Unity has taught me that the power and the presence of God dwells within me. I loved the way the late Maya Angelou (a student of Unity) put it when she said on Super Soul Sunday with Oprah Winfrey, "God Loves Me." That's right and God is Love. This is why I named this chapter "Love is my Religion" because I refuse to follow any teaching that does not teach the truth about God, which is God is Love.

Let's take an in-depth look at the five basic principles of Unity to grasp how powerful they are when we apply them to our lives.

*1 - God is the source and creator of all. There is no other enduring power. God is good and present everywhere.*

If you truly believe that God is the source and creator of all, imagine what type of freedom that gives your life. Should you ever worry about anything? No!! God's got it... God is the source and the creator of all.

If the economy is in a recession (so say the economist), so what? The economy is not your source, God is! If the doctor gives you two months to live, so what? The doctor can only give a diagnosis. Only God can give a prognosis! Just got laid off from your job? So what? Your job is not your source of income; God is! Remember, it's God's money anyway.

*There is no other enduring power.* In other words, just like when Moses asked God "Who shall I say sent me when I go to the Israelites? God replied "Tell them I AM has sent you." Powerful statement and so true. Basically, God is saying there is no name that I need to go by. I Am that I Am. And, of course, you are that as well.

*God is good and present everywhere.* God is Omnipresence- in all things, in all places, at all times. That God is in you and me. The presence of the I AM dwells within you: The Christ Within. That is a powerful concept to truly grasp and know. Ye are Gods.

2 - *We are spiritual beings, created in God's image. The spirit of God lives within each person; therefore, all people are inherently good.*

Think about that. If God is good and we are made in the image and likeness of God, then we must be inherently good as well. Why would the good book say we are made in the image and likeness of God if we weren't like God? It makes no sense. We are like God; in fact, we are just like God; we just don't know it. Jesus knew it. He knew who he was and he spent his short time here on earth trying to convince us of who we were, as well. Remember, "you, too, will do these things and even greater." This is important to know and understand. We are not born of sin. We are not inherently evil. We are inherently good just like our heavenly Father/Mother God...

3 - *We create our life experiences through our way of thinking.*

As a man thinketh, so he becomes. That's right, this isn't "new thought" its old thought! This idea has been around for centuries and it is true. We create our reality by the way that we think. Let me give you an example: If you think that smoking is cool and you enjoy doing it because "everyone else is doing it", then you will create a reality where, for you, smoking is a necessity. You will congregate with people who smoke and hang out in places where smokers go, maybe to a cigar bar, for example, or the smoker's section at the airport. On the other hand, if you think that smoking is bad than your reality would be very different. You would congregate with people who don't smoke. Your choices for going out would be totally different than someone who smokes. You may choose to hang out at the art studio or inside the restaurant where smoking is not allowed. I'm not saying either reality is right or wrong. What I'm saying is that your realities would be very different. I can speak from my own experience. In my earlies 20's and 30's, I smoked cigarettes and my reality was completely different than it is NOW. I mean, I couldn't imagine a weekend without an ice-cold Corona and a pack of Marlboro Lights! I had no problem being in the smoke-filled club on a Saturday night. NOW the last place I want to be is in a club or bar filled with smoke. I'd rather stay home. Different way of thinking; different reality.

4 - *There is power in affirmative prayer, which we believe increases our awareness of God.*

Yes, all prayer works. Even the begging pleading prayer to a God that is "up there" in the sky somewhere. However affirmative prayer is even more powerful. Why? Because affirmative prayer is not praying *to* God but praying *from* the God that is within you. Think of it this way, when you are praying *to* God, you are praying to a power outside of yourself. When you are praying *from* God you are praying from the Christ within, which is the power that exists within you. This type of prayer inherently increases your awareness of the God power that exists within you. It's a good thing.

5 - *Knowledge of these spiritual principles is not enough. We must live them.*

This is an obvious one however many people miss it. You can read all the books you want and take all the classes. If you don't live these principles though you will not experience their true power. If you think that knowing these principles makes you better than someone else, well then, you are missing the point of the five basic principles in the first place. To live them is to know that you are just as important and awesome as every other living creature on this planet. Knowing them is easy. Living them takes effort and hard work. That is the key. This speaks to the point of preachers preaching the gospel versus preaching what Jesus taught. In many churches today you may find the minister preaching "the Gospel of Jesus Christ." There is only one problem; they are not teaching what Jesus taught. They are not teaching the example of what Jesus lived. I love the slogan that came out years ago. You remember WWJD. What Would Jesus Do? That is a great slogan because it brings us back to the truth of what Jesus was teaching and living at the time. Jesus taught us to love one another as he said in John 13:34 - *A new command I give you: Love one another. As I have loved you, so you must love one another."* As our Way Shower, Jesus not only talked the talk, he walked the walked as demonstrated by his many works throughout the bible.

## *Physically - Spiritually - Financially*

If you have a **physical** ailment that is troubling you, maybe the reason you have not been cured is because you aren't loving it enough! We've been fighting cancer for 50 years but we still don't have a cure. I think it's time we started loving Cancer to find the cure. I have a friend who is strong and courageous and she has shared her journey with Cancer for the past couple of years. The interesting thing about her is, instead of dreading the treatments and running away from them, she has chosen to love the treatments, the nurses, the bags of medicine, and everything that goes along with her journey and treatment. In fact, she often sings about it and posts her journey on Facebook and other forms of social media. It is truly refreshing to see someone show love to her body and the medication she is taking to help heal it. I see her whole and healthy as she continues on her journey. The key is love. Love your broken bones as they heal, love your hurt back as the pain subsides, love your sinuses as you deal with allergies. Love yourself back to health and set yourself free.

Does your religion feel less like love and more like hate? Does your religion teach you that you must not associate with certain people because of their religious affiliation, race, ethnicity, sexual orientation? Does your religion teach you that women are not capable of leading the church? Does your religion teach that, if you don't follow said religion, then you are going to hell? If any of the above apply, then you need a new religion. Our differences are what makes us stronger, not weaker. Our differences are what makes us all unique. This is why I consider myself spiritual, not religious. **Spirituality** deals with experience whereas religion deals with dogma. If you feel your life is lacking love, you may want to consider losing your religion. Connect with the I AM inside of you and feel the presence of God. This is where you find true freedom. When you experience that bliss, there is nothing left to be said. Spirituality is the experience of you and the divine and there is no love greater than that.

Are the bills tight every month? Living paycheck to paycheck? Have you ever considered that you are not loving yourself enough to take a chance? To leap off the cliff into the unknown? Fear can definitely stop you from loving yourself enough to take control of your finances. Some people live the same year for 25 years and call it a life. I call that insanity! If you want to change your finances, start by loving yourself enough to know that you must change something. Love that you are going to start saving money. Love that you are opening a new business bank account. Love that you are taking that new seminar on financial intelligence. This isn't about loving money, this is about loving yourself and the ability to change your circumstances. When you love yourself enough to know you deserve better, you will change your life forever and truly set yourself free. Love yourself back into financial stability and onward to **financial** freedom.

## No matter the Question, Love is the Answer

If you want to become Physically, Spiritually and Financially free reconnect yourself with love in every aspect of your life. Our great Way Shower, Jesus, taught us best when he shared these two great commandments... *Jesus said unto him, Thou shalt love the Lord, thy God, with all thy heart, and with all thy soul, and with all thy mind.*

*This is the first and **great commandment**. And the second is, like unto it, Thou shalt love thy neighbor as thyself. On these two **commandments** hang all the law and the prophets.*

No matter what valley you may be traveling through, know that this too shall pass. No matter how hard the times get, know that this too shall pass. No matter how much hatred you may see in the world, know that this too shall pass. No matter how dark it gets, know that this too shall pass. The late Dr. MLK Jr. said it best when he said "Darkness cannot drive out darkness, only light can do that. Hate cannot drive out hate. Only love can do that." And where there is love there is no darkness.

# *What Can I Do NOW?*

**I** - Practice Random acts of Kindness

I challenge you to just a pick a day and pay for the person's coffee behind you in line. Pay for the person's toll in the toll booth. Pay for the person's meal in the drive-thru. Showing random acts of kindness is a powerful tool to open up your heart to unconditional love.

**II** - Take a deep look at your religion and your religious practices. Ask yourself these questions?

1. Why did I join the religion that I'm a part of NOW? Was I born into it? Did I leave another religion to join my current one?
2. Does my religion teach unconditional love? How?
3. If not, what does my religion teach about love? Does this match what Jesus taught and lived?

4. Does my religion single any one group, or groups, out and say they are not worthy of God's love or not worthy of going to "Heaven", or the Promised Land, or receiving salvation?" Analyze your answers. Ask yourself, is love my religion?

# Chapter III - "Do you understand the words that are coming out of my mouth?"

*"The effectiveness of communication is not defined by the communication, but by the response."* - Milton Erickson

What is key about this quote from Milton Erickson? He uses the word "effective" communication. Of course we all communicate all the time in many different ways; verbally, written, and through body language. The question is how effective is our communication?

Anyone who wants to be successful at anything must communicate effectively. Take any product or service company, you will notice that the great ones know how to communicate with their customers. Have you ever wondered why McDonalds still does commercials? I mean, everyone knows who they are. Couldn't they just stop doing commercials and save that money? Wouldn't people still continue to go to McDonalds anyway? The answer is no, they wouldn't. McDonald's executives know that they must continue to innovate and come up with new products and services and, then, communicate their message to their customers on an ongoing basis if they want to keep their customers and gain new ones. The same goes for Nike. We all know what Nike is so why does Nike have so many commercials?

Because the executives at Nike know they must continue to innovate and share their brand message with their customers if they want to continue their success as a company. These are just two prime examples of effective communication in the business world. The results, of course, show up in the response. Have you visited the Golden Arches lately or bought any item with that famous Swoosh? Chances are you have.

So, what about us? Why is effective communication so important to us and how can it lead us to becoming Physically, Spiritually and Financially free? Well, the concept is the same. If you want to be successful in your life, then you must communicate effectively with your customers. Who are your customers? Your family, friends, co-workers, acquaintances, husband, wife, children and, of course, yourself. Anyone that you come in contact with is your customer in life. The more effectively you communicate with them, the better off your life will be. Let's discuss some of these relationships in detail.

*Your friends* - Most of us already know that it is important to have good communication with our friends. Actually, for some of us we may communicate better with our friends than we do with our own family. Yes, it happens. Regardless, the communication factor is important. Have you ever had that best friend that you felt you could tell anything to? Sure, we all have. That person and that relationship is/was one of the most important relationships in your life. Why?

Because you trusted he or she and he or she trusted you. Communication is easy when you have that kind of trust. Therefore, the relationship is easy. On the other hand, what about a friend that you lost touch with, but all of a sudden out of the blue they call you and want to "catch up?" Maybe this friend was your drinking buddy back in college and, now, you don't drink anymore. Communication might get a little tougher in this situation because you don't have that connection with them anymore and you know some of your priorities and habits have changed. I've experienced this myself. Back when I was a heavy partier and drinker I had friends that I hung out with all the time. We would all meet up at the house together and down a couple of beers and/or shots before heading off to the club for the night. You know the pre-party. After one of my many attempts to quit drinking, I remember heading over to the house for a pre-party, as we usually did, but I was not going to drink. I recall drinking Gatorade instead of beer and still attempted to have a good time. It didn't work out too well for me. The party was going on all around me and I felt so out of place. It was like I was in a twilight zone. Everyone was having such a great time and I was just there watching it happen instead of being a part of it. Have you ever been the only sober person at a party? It's a weird feeling. Since I didn't communicate with my friends what I was attempting to do, they weren't there as a support system for me. Don't get me wrong. It wasn't their fault. It was my fault for not realizing that I didn't communicate clearly what I was attempting to do. In hindsight the best option for communication for me in this situation would have been to tell my friends that I needed some time away from the party scene to get myself together. Had I done that, I'm sure they would have supported me in that effort. Eventually, I did just that. Communicating clearly what I wanted to do and effectively implementing that plan helped change my life forever. The great part about it is, I still have these people in my life as friends. We may not hang out or see each other as much, but I still consider them friends.

*Your Spouse* - You and your spouse / significant other need great communication for the relationship to last. I know, as well as anybody, that this is not easy. My wife and I certainly have our times when we don't see things the same way. This is normal for everyone. It reminds me of that book, "Men are from Mars and Women are from Venus." It's true, men and women communicate differently. So, it's important that we make a concerted effort to understand each other in order to have effective communication.

## *Cinnamon and Sugar*

We have two cats, Cinnamon and Sugar. Let's just get this straight right out of the box. I'm not crazy about cats. I don't hate 'em and I don't love 'em. It's just what it is. I remember having cats while growing up and playing with them as a kid, but somehow, in my older years, I've become allergic to them. I can't touch them or I start to itch all over my body. Maybe, this is why I'm not crazy about cats these days. When Amy and I met she already had Cinnamon and Sugar, so they are a part of the family. We agreed we would keep the cats out of the bedroom when we moved into our new home because we didn't want any accidents on the carpet and because I'm allergic to cats. As time went on, though, slowly the cats started to make their way into our bedroom. After about two months Amy would have them laying on the bed with her when I would get home. A couple more months passed and the cats would be sleeping in the room with Amy during an afternoon nap. Now, there's a water bowl for the kitty sitting next to our shower! So what happened? I'm not going to say that I'm happy about this, but it's a great test for working on communication in a relationship. I'm not saying it's easy. I'm saying it's a work in progress. At first, I would get upset when the cats were laying on the bed in our room. Now, I don't say anything about it. Amy has agreed that the cats must go before we go to bed. Amy and I have talked about it. She expressed to me how she grew up with her cats sleeping in the bed with her, so it's a huge change for her not to have the cats be in the bedroom. It's just one example of a little give and take when it comes to communication.  It's kinda funny because, as soon as I go into the room, Sugar knows it's time for her to leave. She just jumps off the bed and heads out the door without me even asking -most of the time. Effective communication. We talked it out and are making it work for us. That is the key.

*Your Children* - Any parent knows that communicating with your children is a challenge. Let me tell you from experience, when they get older (in most cases, and certainly in mine), it becomes more difficult to communicate effectively with them because they are starting to make their own decisions and come into their own as an adult. This is a difficult time as a parent because they are still so vulnerable. Science says that the brain is not fully developed until a person is about 25 years old. So, if you're not there yet just hold on parents! "Keep 'em alive 'til 25" and you are a scot-free! Well not quite, but you get the picture. The quality of your communication with them while they are young will help determine how well your communication will be when they get older.

### *Lil T and Yaya*

I remember taking them to church on Sundays when my kids were much younger, then coming home and enjoying a Sunday afternoon at the park. We always had fun on our weekends together. I always kept our lines of communication as open as I thought they could be. I remember sitting in church one morning and the minister asked if anyone remembers something that a parent taught them when they were younger. He was directing the question to the adults in the room, however, my son raised his hand to answer the question. Lil T must have been 10 or so at the time. T promptly said, "You either do or you don't, there is no try." I was proud because I knew I had been teaching them both that for a long time. Something must have been sticking. I thought I was doing pretty good with this whole communication thing. But, things get trickier as they get older. Like the day I pulled up to pick them up from their grandmother's house and I'm told my son is no longer a virgin. (He was 16 at the time.) I thought, "Wait a minute! We never even had "the conversation!" What happened to all that communication that I was gleaming about earlier? I guess I missed the boat on this one. Newsflash! Turns out your teenagers don't want to tell you everything that is going on in their lives. So, after the fact, T and I had that conversation about the birds and the bees. It was just as awkward for him as it was for me. I remember him saying "I can't believe we're having this conversation." We got through it though and we're better for it.

Then there's the day I was at work and I got a call from their mother saying it's an emergency and I have to call her back right away. I call her back and she explains to me that Yaniece told her she thinks she's attracted to women instead of men. Her Mother was in a frenzy about this and asked what should we do? I said, we're going to love her just the same. She's our daughter and nothing has changed." For me, it didn't come as a shock, even though Yaniece and I had never had a conversation about it. Yaniece, even as very young girl never wanted to wear makeup or dresses or anything like that. It just was never part of her personality; Frankly I wasn't surprised. I calmed her Mother down and we moved on. When it came time for Yaniece to go to the prom, I picked her and her girlfriend up and drove them to the prom. Yaniece was dressed in a sweet looking tuxedo and her date in a beautiful dress. We took some great pictures that night and they had a wonderful time. I'm confident that Yaniece feels comfortable talking to me about her relationship. I feel comfortable talking with her, as well. It's all about keeping those lines of communication open and communicating effectively.

*Your Acquaintances* - Effective communication with acquaintances is extremely important. Who are these people? Pretty much anyone that is not a friend or family member - your garbage man, the customer service rep on the phone, your co-workers, that random stranger in Walmart or at the bank. You never know who that stranger might be. Today, they are a stranger in Walmart. Next week you could be sitting in front of them at a job interview and they are the decision maker. It's happened before. Always treat people with kindness and respect and it will be given right back to you. Here's the key, it may not come back to you from the person that you want it to come from, but, it will come back to you. Pay attention to the Universe and you will see. The Universe always says yes. The challenge is, we don't always know what we are asking for. If we ask, though, and know in our heart that it is already done, the Universe responds in kind.

## The Parable of the Sower

Have you ever read the Parable of the Sower? Matthew 13: 1-8. It is an excellent example of effective communication with the Universe. The Farmer plants some seed. He lays the first bit of seed, but before it even gets a chance to grow the birds eat it. He then lays some more seed which this time lands on rocky ground. Some of the seeds started to grow, but the soil was too shallow. When the sun came out, they all withered and died. The farmer plants some more seed. This time it lands on thorny ground. Again, some of the seeds start to grow, but the thorns rise up and choke them. They all die. However, undeterred, the farmer plants some more seed and this time it lands on fertile ground. The crops produce 30, 60 and 100 times what was sown.

The Farmer knew that, if he kept sewing his excellent seed, he would eventually be rewarded for his efforts. You, my friend, are just like that farmer. Keep sowing your excellent seed. Don't get deterred when the birds, the sun, or the thorns get some of it. Keep sowing. Eventually, your crops will flourish. Keep positive thoughts. Stay connected with that all knowing power of the Universe. This is the ultimate example of effective communication and connecting with source.

## Yourself

Last, but not least, you must have effective communication with yourself. Do you know that you talk to yourself all the time? Well, you do. Most of us are our own worst critics and we tend to talk negatively about ourselves all the time. This is all done, for the most part, subconsciously. We don't even realize we are doing it. I was recently watching a video on YouTube. This guy was covering a song and, right at the beginning of the video, he says, "I don't know if this is gonna be any good or not but you can watch it if you want to." He had less than a thousand views. I wonder why? I'm sure he didn't mean to deter people from watching his video, but, in effect, that's what he was doing. He didn't think he was any good. He was saying it to his possible viewers before he even started to perform. We must learn how important our self-talk is to our lives.

## Self-Talk

What is your self-talk?? Your self-talk is how you talk to yourself. If you take the time to get into a quiet space, you can hear it. We are all constantly in a conversation with ourselves. The question becomes, who are we listening to? The ego will always want to drive you back to safety while your higher self will want to push you out of the airplane and grow your wings on the way down. I remember leading worship for the first time at Unity North Tampa and feeling nervous. I felt the fear running through my body before I had to get up and introduce Sounds of Light and our first song. How was I going to sing? How was I was going to play guitar? My palms were getting sweaty and I had jitters in my stomach. I quickly went to my self-talk and said "Hey you are more than capable of doing this. You've done this before for years at your previous church. NOW is no different. Calm down, take three deep breaths and let's do this." And I did just that. NOW every morning I look in the mirror and I say to myself "I AM a super creator and a magnet for attracting the things I want in my life." It's an affirmation that gets me started every day and it works for me. I recommend using affirmations to continually keep your self-talk positive. Post them up on your bathroom mirror. Put them in the kitchen. Put them in your car or on your phone as a meeting reminder. Yes, I do that! Whatever it takes to keep your self- talk positive. Effective, positive communication with yourself is one of the keys to living a happy, healthy life. It will most certainly set you free.

## *Physically - Spiritually - Financially*

Do you have a nagging injury or some **physical** ailment that won't go away? I'm a runner and I remember when I was training for the Twin Cities Marathon in 2012. I spent the entire year training for this race. Then came up with a nasty case of runner's knee right before the race. I canceled my flight and didn't do the race. What was the problem? How did I feel perfectly fine one day and then couldn't run 50 feet without excruciating pain the next? Simple. Communication. The truth is my body was giving me signals all the time. I just wasn't listening. I needed more rest. I was running too many miles without icing and stretching properly. I wasn't getting sports massages like I should have. So, slowly over time, my body just said enough is enough and shut down.  Had I been aware and communicating effectively with my body, I would have seen the signs of fatigue before it was too late and prevented all the pain that I had to go through.  If you're dealing with a physical ailment, I challenge you to get to a quiet space. Get in tune with your body and communicate with it effectively. You will be surprised what you will notice. Am I saying don't go see a doctor? No, to the contrary, I'm saying once you get in tune with your body you may realize that's exactly what you need to do. Go see a doctor to get the help and treatment that you need. That peace of mind will set you free.

**Spirituality** is all about effective communication with your higher self - with the Christ within. In Unity, we believe in a God that lives within us. We are already connected with this spirit because it is a part of who we are. If you ever feel disconnected, it's because you have moved away (subconsciously) from the God spirit that you are. God didn't move.  How do you get that connection back? Prayer and Meditation. Find that quiet space. Get in touch with your higher self. Then listen. When you are there, you will know. Remember, the Universe always says yes, so our job is to be sure of what we are asking. Effective communication in spirituality starts with affirmative prayer. Pray from God not to God. When you pray from your God self you are strengthening that connection between you and the Christ within. That will certainly set you free.

Who's in control of your **finances**? You are! Sit down and figure out your spending plan for the month. Notice I didn't say budget because budget sounds so restricting. I figure out my spending plan months in advance and then I work my plan. This is an example of effective communication with myself. If you have a spouse and/or significant other, you must communicate with each other to manage your finances for the household. I recommend sitting down each month and going over the finances for the home. Plan for expenses that only come up once a year, as well as for vacations and trips. The more you plan the better. I love the quote by Alan Lakein, "Planning is bringing the future into the present so that you can do something about it NOW." Planning is a major part of effective communication. If you do it well, it will make your life that much better and set you free

### *Communication is Key*

If you want to lead a life where you are Physically, Spiritually and Financially free, you must turn yourself into an expert communicator. The art of communication is the language of leadership. All great leaders are great communicators. Think about all the people you interact with on a daily basis - spouse, friends, family, acquaintances, and, most importantly, yourself. Are you communicating in the most effective way with these people? Be cognizant of your self-talk. How well are you communicating with yourself? Ask yourself what you are saying to yourself all the time. Are you lifting yourself up or putting yourself down? What results have you been attracting in your life? What response are you receiving from the Universe? After all the effectiveness of communication is not defined by the communication, but by the response.

# *What Can I Do NOW?*

I - Suggested reading – <u>Non-violent Communication</u> by Marshall B. Rosenberg PhD. This book has great teachings and exercises on how to implement effective communication techniques in your relationships. This is an amazing book that everyone should have in their library. It certainly is a part of my library.

II - Find a speaking group and join. A few examples would be Toastmasters or the National Speakers Association. Both are great for getting started in the direction of more effective communication. You can find them online. I have experience as a member of Toastmasters. I can truly say that the lessons that I've learned in Toastmasters have made a huge impact on my life.

# Chapter IV - "Do I really have to jump?"

"Everything you want is on the other side of fear." - Jack Canfield

Yes! You do. You do have to jump. The above quote by Jack Canfield is so powerful. Literally everything that you want is for the taking but you have to get past the fear first. I love the saying "In order to get to something, you have to go through something". I was recently watching a video on YouTube of the comedian Steve Harvey talking about taking the leap of faith. He's so right. To achieve anything in life, you must take a leap of faith. As Dr. Martin Luther King once said, "You have to take the first step in faith; you don't have to see the whole staircase." Most people go through life afraid to live. Afraid to move. Afraid to take any chances. Afraid to take any risk. The amazing thing is though, the biggest risk you can ever take in life is not taking any risk at all. There is a difference between being cautious and being fearful. Caution allows you to move forward being careful with every step, whereas fear paralyzes you and you are unable to move at all. Be cautious but not fearful.

Wisdom tells us there are only two emotions... Love and Fear. To take it a step further, we are born with only two innate fears:

1) The fear of loud noises

2) The fear of falling

That's right, babies only fear loud noises and falling off something. So where do all these fears that we have come from? You guessed it. They're learned. Who do we learn them from? Right again. Our parents. Who did our parents learn them from? Their parents! And so on and so on. A never ending cycle. This isn't to say that a healthy amount of fear isn't important. Of course, it is. A healthy amount of fear stops us from burning ourselves on the stove or walking in front of traffic or falling off the bike (sometimes). It's the unhealthy amount of fear that is the challenge though. An unhealthy amount of fear can paralyze us and leave us unable to move forward in life.

*Sink or Swim*

When I was 9 or 10 years old, I remember going to the neighborhood pool. It was a beautiful hot summer day in Florida. I woke up feeling the hot sun coming through my tiny bedroom window. As I went out to play that day, my friends, Mike, Babra, and Chris told me they were going to the pool and asked if my brother, Michael, and I wanted to join them. I was the youngest of the group, so their mom, Mrs. Kitty, said to ask my mother first if I could go. If she said yes then we could ride down with them. Off I went, sprinting back home, I asked my mom if I could go to the pool she smiled and said yes with a stiff warning to remind me to be careful up there. My brother and I said, "Of course" and we left.

It was a perfect day for the pool. The sun was out and everyone was enjoying themselves. The smell of chlorine and bbq filled the air. Over on one side, there was a group of guys playing basketball on the basketball court, and, over to the left, the kids were playing foursquare and tether ball. The pool sat in middle and was surrounded by everyone and everything. I was just sitting on the side of the pool, watching the kids in the pool playing "MARCO... POLO... MARCO... POLO.... MARCO.... POLO." As I sat there, one of the neighborhood pranksters, we will call him Willie, decided he wanted to play a prank on me. So, as I sat there enjoying the scenery and the game of Marco Polo, Willie crept up behind me and, before I knew it, he grabbed me and threw me in the deep end of the pool. I remember screaming with horror as I was heading towards the water and hearing Willie laughing in the background. Splash!!! Down I went. As I was slowly sinking, I could still hear the Marco Polo game going on around me MARCO... POLO... MARCO...POLO. As I went deeper and deeper, it turned into a faint whisper "marco... polo.... marco.... polo.... marc......"

You see, what Willie didn't know as he was pulling off his awesome prank was I didn't know how to swim! Thank God there was someone there who recognized what had happened. Billy, Kitty's husband, was over at the grill and saw Willie throw me in the pool. Billy jumped into action and dove into the pool to save me. Had Billy not acted as quickly as he did, I surely would have drowned that day. He saved my life. I tell this story to make a point. I still remember the feeling of going under water, trying to breathe, but not being able to. I remember the fear I felt as I continued to consume water (not air) as I sunk to the bottom of that pool. To this day, 35 years later, I still don't know how to swim because of the fear of that memory. I just have the hardest time sticking my head below the water. That's how powerful fear can be. If I ever want to do that Ironman Triathlon race I'm going to have to get past this fear. I will get there; I know I will. So will you. No matter what, you must not let fear win.

## *Love*

Every emotion ultimately is an offspring of Love. So, basically, there is only one emotion… L.O.V.E.

Let me explain what I mean.

**Fear** - In my example about fear of drowning, the ultimate truth is I love my life and that is why I "fear" drowning. If a Mother says she fears for her child's safety, in reality, what she is saying is she loves her child and doesn't want her to get hurt. We had a small snake in our front yard last night and, even though it was small, we didn't know whether it was poisonous or not. So, Amy and I told the kids to stay away from it. Of course, the real reason we told the kids to stay away from it is because we love our kids and want them to be safe.

**Anger/Frustration-** When I get angry with my kids (which I often do), I'm angry because I love them and I want the best for them. For example, I told Yaniece I wanted her to move in with me sooner rather than later. She was supposed to move in early 2016. Here it is summer 2017 and she hasn't moved in yet. We have an empty room in our house for her, but she hasn't made up her mind yet. Teenagers! Am I angry, or maybe a better word is frustrated, at the situation? Yes, I am. But, why am I frustrated? Because I love my daughter, I want the best for her, and I feel that her moving in with me would be the best for her. Of course, ultimately, the decision is and always has been up to her.

**Sadness** - When you feel sad what are you really feeling? When my Father passed away, I can still remember walking down the aisle in that church towards the body as we were going to take our seat. My father's casket lay in front of us. All I remember is I couldn't hold back the tears. It just didn't seem right. It didn't seem real that he was gone and I felt so sad about it. Was I feeling sadness or was I feeling love? I was feeling the love that I had for my Father and all those memories were going through my head at once. I'm sure many of you have been there before, too.

**Depressed** - When you feel depressed, you are feeling the love that you think is missing from your life. Some people get depressed because someone or something in their life is gone. For instance, someone dies, a parent or spouse. The truth is you are missing the love that you had for that person. Some people get depressed when they lose their car. Hey, it happens. But, the principle is the same. You are not depressed. You are missing the love you felt for that car. It's all about Love...

All emotions are an offset of Love. Here's the good news. We are never separate from that Love because that is who we are. L.O.V.E.

The **L** in love stands for Life- We are the life of God. God lives through us. So, what is life? Life is the condition that distinguishes animals and plants from inorganic matter including the capacity for growth, reproduction, functional activity and continual change preceding death.

> **Growth:** Yes, we have the ability to grow, not just as we age, but also through our experiences. We are continually learning and growing until our death. **Reproduction**: We have the ability to reproduce and, of course, we must do this to keep our species alive on this planet.
>
> **Functional Activity:** We must stay active, active in our minds, body, and spirit. This means physical activity and spiritual activity.
>
> **Continual Change:** Everything changes all the time and that

includes us. Our bodies are continually changing. Scientists say we have a completely new body of skin every three years.

**Preceding death:** Of course, we know that what we call "death" is simply a transition back into our spiritual form. Yes, we are the Life of God in expression.

The **O** in love stands for Omnipresence. We are the Omnipresence of God. Have you ever thought, "How does God show up in our world?" Omnipresence means being present everywhere at the same time. How does God do that? Simple. We are that presence. As Eddie Watkins Jr. put in one of his songs "I am the place where God shows up." We are the Omnipresence in action.

The **V** in love stands for Verity. Verity means truth. The truth is we are made in the image and likeness of God. We have the Christ spirit within us. That is why Jesus said, "You will do these things I do and even greater." Believe that because it is the truth about you.

The **E** in love stands for Expectation - Expectation is another way of saying Faith. We are the Faith of God. When we show faith, we are allowing others to see what God can do. Some people say seeing is believing. Well, that's not true. Believing is seeing. Expect God to do great things in your life and She will.

# *Physically - Spiritually - Financially*

Have you ever been afraid that you can't accomplish a **physical** task? Maybe a sport that you play? When I was 30 years old I decided I wanted to run a marathon. So, I put my name in the lottery for the NYC marathon. Now, mind you, I had never run a marathon before, not even a half marathon! Low and behold, in the summer of 2003, I got the letter in the mail that said I was selected. I would be running the NYC marathon in November of that year. Was I excited? Yes!! Was I scared? Yes!! I didn't know what to do or how to train. I didn't even know how I was going to get there. But, day by day, I started doing the little things to prepare me. I bought a book with training plans. I found a group to run with. I took baby steps and took them one at a time. Eventually, I found myself crossing the finish line of the NYC marathon an experience I will never forget. I would never have experienced that feeling had I not overcome my fear of completing a marathon. The key is this, my friend. It doesn't matter if it's running a marathon or walking down your block, when you feel that fear creeping into your consciousness, it's ok to acknowledge that it's there, but do it anyway! As long as it's not illegal, do it! Do the thing you fear and the death of fear is certain. The way you get past your fears is to take small steps that eventually get you to where you want to be. If you do this, you will conquer your fears. That will set you free.

Are you afraid of what you think God is? Or afraid of what other people may think about your **Spirituality**? First of all, God is Love, so how could you ever be afraid of that? If someone is preaching to you that you should be afraid of God, move away as fast as you possibly can. There is nothing to fear when it comes to God. Now, if you are afraid of what others feel about your Spirituality, then you should ask yourself why you feel that way. What is there to be ashamed of? There are roughly 4200 different religions in the world, so, trust me, no matter what you believe there is always going to be someone who believes something different from you. It's not a bad thing either. It's a good thing. As a proud Unity student, I am happy to discuss my beliefs about Unity and how its teachings have changed my life. However, I don't feel the need to tell someone they have to believe what I believe. I have no fear about it because I don't have to convince someone to change what they believe. There are many paths to the same home. Whenever you feel scared about what your belief system is and how it might offend someone else, just remember there are at least 4199 other religions out there for someone to get mad about. That should make you feel better.

If your money is funny and you fear you are not going to make it to the next check. Approach your fear on a step by step basis. First, determine why you are having money problems. I recently was at a seminar where the speaker was teaching about compound interest and how it works to build wealth. He asked the group, "Have you ever heard the statement 'the rich get richer and the poor get poorer'?" We all said, of course, we have heard it before. He said, "Well it's true. Poor people continue to learn bad money habits from their parents and repeat the same cycle. Whereas, rich people learn good money habits from their parents and repeat the cycle." Poor people save money, rich people invest money. That's the difference. If you came from a home like mine then your mom told you to get a good paying job and save your money in a bank. If you came from a rich family, your mother would have told you to create a company of your own and invest your money in real estate, stocks, bonds and mutual funds. Two very different teachings. So, if you find yourself having money troubles and it seems there is no way out, ask yourself this question, "Am I repeating the same mistakes that my parents taught me?" Whose advice am I taking when it comes to money and how I handle it? Here's some steps to take. Find a trusted friend who's rich already (not a poor friend; that won't help) and ask him or her how he or she did it. If you don't have a rich friend, then read the books of rich people. They all tell you how they did it. It's a matter of listening and following the blueprint. And, by the way, many of the books you can get for free in the library. If you want to be **financially** free, the first thing you must do is learn how to invest your money.

## *Face Your Fears*

Fear is one of the most paralyzing forces on earth. If you want to accomplish anything in life, you must be able to overcome your fears.

The basic rules to overcoming fear are simple. They are... Recognize what the fear is; take appropriate action steps to overcome the fear in a methodical pattern; realize that the very thing you fear just might be your calling. If you are just dying to get on stage and belt out that song at open mic night, BUT you are afraid - you probably are meant to be on that stage. If you know you should be running your own business, BUT you are too afraid to leave your job - you probably should be your own boss. If you just know you can complete that Ironman, BUT you fear swimming - you probably should be doing an Ironman. Yeah, that last one was for me. Remember, your true calling and what will really set you free is right there for the taking because everything you want is on the other side of fear.

# *What Can I Do NOW?*

## I - Face your Fears

This is the simplest and most effective way to overcome fear. You must face them. I cannot tell you how many times I've dreaded doing something because of fear and, when I did it, it turned out to be nothing compared to what I had conjured up in my mind.

Pick one of your smaller fears. Find an accountability partner that you trust and will help you get through this. Do the thing you fear. This exercise helps you build the courage to face your fears. Start with baby steps and, then, you will build the courage to go after the larger fears that may be holding you back.

## II - Contemplation Station

Write down on a piece of paper three of your biggest fears. Now ask yourself these questions. Write down your answers and meditate on them. Meditate on your answers daily. While you're in the silence, the answers of what you should do will be revealed to you.

> 1) What is the worst thing that could happen if my biggest fear came true? What's the best thing that could happen if my

biggest fear came true?

2) Would I be less of a person if this happened? Would I be more of a person if this happened?

3) Would my family and friends still love me if this happened? Would my family and friends love me more if this happened?

4) Will this even matter 3, 5, 10, 15, 20, 30, 50 years from NOW? (If the answer is no, then why worry about it NOW?)

# **Chapter V - Control what you can control**

"Lack of direction, not lack of time, is the problem. We all have twenty-four hour days." – Zig Ziglar

Everyone must manage their time. But how do you do that? How do you control time when it seems to be uncontrollable? Think about it. No matter what we do time will continue to move on nonstop and there is nothing we can do about it. Time is out of our control. There are many different things one can do to manage their time more wisely and in this chapter we are going to discuss a few of them. But first I have to let you in on a little secret...

## **There's no such thing as Time Management!**

Oh you make think you are managing your time when you plan out your day from 9am meeting to 1pm lunch to 7pm basketball practice and everything else in between. But the truth is you are managing yourself not your time.

The only thing we can truly manage is ourselves. That's right I said it and it's the truth. So this chapter is about Self-Management. Self-Management is key to living a fulfilling life. So how do we manage ourselves?

## *Marathon Running*

I'm training to run the Marine Corps Marathon this year. The race is October 22nd 2017. I'm super excited! This will be my sixth marathon. Every one of them have been a challenge and a triumph. From NYC back in 2003 all the way up to Philly in 2016. The one thing I remember about them all is that it took an enormous amount of discipline to train for running the 26.2 mile distance. Anyone who has ever run a marathon knows this. It takes discipline to work your way through the training for the race. It takes discipline to eat healthy. It takes discipline to abstain from drinking and partying late. It takes discipline to get up every day early in the morning or running late at night just to get all of your mileage in. Have there been times when I've been less disciplined than others in my training? Yes, it sure has. Did it affect my marathon? It sure did. I can recall running the Philly marathon in November 2016. I remember it was a super cold windy morning (27 degrees F) and as I passed the 20 mile mark I could not believe I still had 6.2 miles to go. I had definitely hit "the wall." I could barely feel my legs and the wind was brutally whipping at my face. Even though I was covered up in layers I could still feel the sting of the wind as it barreled towards me and all of my fellow running mates out there. As for my hands, well I had just bought gloves the night before at the expo but it felt as if I had nothing on at all. I couldn't imagine going another 6 miles in that weather. It was grueling and it was painful, but I did it because I really wanted to finish. NOW contrast that to when I ran the Twin Cities Marathon in October 2012. The temperature was nearly identical as in Philly, (about 27 degrees). This race I can specifically remember crossing the 20 mile mark and saying to myself "Wow I can't believe I feel this good! I'm not hitting the wall." Just in case you're wondering the 20 mile mark of the marathon is the imaginary place where many runners say they hit "the wall." The wall is when you start feeling the true fatigue in your legs and it gets tougher to move them forward. The wall is when the lactic acid has built up in your muscle and they are no longer firing. The wall is when you catch that cramp in your quad that feels like a rock sitting in your leg. In other words you don't want to hit the wall. What was the difference in the two races? Why did I hit the wall in one and not in the other? There is one clear answer. Discipline! I was much more disciplined in my training for Twin Cities than I was in my training for Philly. And it showed. So why is this so important? It's important because many people are struggling at life because of the same thing. Many people are hitting the wall in life because they are not exercising discipline over themselves. I love the quote…" People suffer one of two pains in life. The pain of discipline or the pain of regret. The difference is discipline weighs ounces and regret weighs tons." In order to manage your time you must manage yourself. In order to manage yourself you must have discipline.

So how do we learn to be disciplined? Here are 3 key steps to help you learn how to be disciplined in your life.

## *Clarity*

1) Figure out what you really want. In other words have clarity about what it is you want to achieve. This is a key step to being disciplined in life. If you don't know what you want or where you want to go how will you ever get there? You cannot be disciplined with your actions when you are not clear on what it is you want. One key step to gaining clarity is this. Write down your goals. Yes I said actually write them down. No, I don't mean type them out (you can do that later). Write them down first. There is something about the power of the physical activity of writing something down that connects with your higher self. It is truly a magnificent thing. When you write these goals down make sure they are specific, time sensitive and write them down as if you have already achieved them. For instance if your goal is to open your own dry cleaning business you would write something like "January 2018 I have opened my business and I am servicing 300 customers per week…" This goal is specific, (300 customers) and time sensitive (January 2018). This method is called working backwards. Choose your goal and map out exactly where you expect to be. Then fill in the details as to how you will get there. For instance in this example… How do you get to 300 customers by January 2018? Well you may have to do some advertising in the local paper, internet, radio

etc. Maybe you start speaking at local events or writing articles pertaining to your industry; create a website or blog. These are the specifics of how you get to your goal and that my friend brings clarity. When you are clear about the steps you need to take to get to where you want to be it makes discipline that much easier.

## *Put in the Work*

2) Put in the work. This ties right in with point number 1. You've got to do the work. You have to go out and promote your business. You have to run the miles. You have to write the lyrics. Whatever your goal is you must put in the work. At this time right NOW I work from 9am to 6pm. I train for my marathon before or after work which means I'm running at 5:30am or 6:30pm. I leave the house at 8am and get home around 9pm every night Monday thru Friday. Once I'm home I shower grab a bite to eat, play with the dog and then around 10pm I head into the studio to record until about 12:30am. Then I go to bed. Wake up around 5:30am and do it all over again. On Saturday mornings while most people are asleep I'm up at 5:30am going out for my long run of 16, 18 or 20 miles. There is no substitute for the work. I cringe every time I see one of those commercials promoting a weight loss product and for the most part they tell people all they have to do is pop this pill or sit there and put this contraption around their waist and they will magically lose weight. It's sad because this could

not be further from the truth. Why do we continue to see products like these? Because they sell, that's why. Why do they sell? Because people want to believe they can get results without putting in the work. There is no substitute for the work. Ask any professional athlete, any successful person in any walk of life and you will see they have a story. I guarantee you they worked extremely hard for years and years before they became an "overnight success." Most people want the glory but they don't know the story. There is no substitute for the work. Commit to putting in the work. This is a cornerstone of discipline.

## *The other 8 hours*

3) We all have 24 hours in a day. The question is what do you choose to do with them? The average American spends anywhere from 3 to 6 hours a day watching television. Is that a good use of your time? I certainly don't believe so. We spend so much of our day either watching TV or on the internet that we barely have time to work on our goals. Think about this; while we are sitting at home watching Basketball, Football, HGTV or Real Housewives of Atlanta what else could we be doing with that time? The people we are watching on TV; they're working. They are getting paid to do what they are doing. And in most cases they are working on their passion, on their dreams, on their goals while we are sitting on the couch eating popcorn or chips watching them and watching the world go by. I remember listening to

the radio one day and a guy made a great point. He said I'm not missing work to watch LeBron James play basketball because I'm pretty sure LeBron James won't miss work to watch me do my job. Think about it. What could you be working on if you took the time you spent watching TV and reallocated it to working on your goals? This is where the other 8 hours comes in. There are 24 hours in a day. On average we spend 8 hours sleeping and 8 hours at work. That's 16 hours. So that leaves us with another 8 hours to do with whatever we please. So let me ask you again. What are you doing with your other 8 hours? Get clear about what you want to achieve, put in the work during that other 8 hours and be disciplined in your approach. If you do this it will change your life.

## Physically – Spiritually – Financially

How are you feeling **physically**? Do you have a physical ailment that is bothering you? Do you feel it is holding you back from achieving your goals in life? Maybe it's time to reevaluate your issue? First and foremost get clear about this issue. Is this something that you should see your doctor about? What work have you put in to bring yourself back to wholeness and health? Have you put in the work? Most times when we suffer from any type of physical ailment it is from neglect over a long period of time. This is why it is so important to stay active throughout your life and continue to exercise as much as you can. If you have a physical ailment, first of all get clarity on the issue. If that entails seeing a physician than do so. Sure, get a few different opinions and then decide for yourself what needs to be done after taking the advice of a medical professional. Once you are clear on the issue then put in the work. If that involves rehabilitation or physical therapy, do that. If it involves changing your diet, do that. You must be disciplined in your approach to your treatment and rehabilitation. This is a key to self-management and managing your health can lead you to a more healthy and happy life and set you free.

Are you lacking discipline in your **spirituality**? Are you saying the peace affirmations in the morning and then blowing up with anger in the afternoon? First of all let me tell you; you are not alone. We are all human and we are not perfect. Everyone goes through this duality. Here are some ways to deal with this challenge. Gain clarity on what you want from your spiritual path. If it's to become closer to God than practice it. Use mindful meditation to get you into that space where you connect with the I AM inside of you. Put in the work. If you are meditating once a day for 5 minutes, up that to 3 times a day for 5 minutes. Then meditate longer. Maybe 15-20 minutes 3 times a day. If you can't seem to find time just use those other 8 hours that you have when you're not sleeping or working... :) And while you're at it use those 8 hours to attend spiritual classes, read books and poems on spirituality and attend Church services. All of these avenues are different ways to find freedom within and strengthen your spirituality. With a little bit of self-management we all can find the time.

How is your financial health? It amazes me that some people will spend hours on their physical health however spend no time on their financial health. Both are extremely important to living a happy and healthy life. Discipline is key when it comes to financial freedom. If you want to experience the bliss of being financially free then you must gain clarity on what it is you want to achieve **financially**. Write out your goals in detail and then work your way backwards figuring out the details of how you will invest your money to become financially free. There's a great book that I read titled "The Millionaire Next Door" and I will never forget some of the knowledge I gained from that book. One of the key points in the book was that the average millionaire in America doesn't drive a fancy car or live in a fancy house. The people who drive the fancy cars and live in the fancy houses are usually broke or just one paycheck away from being broke. They are "keeping up with the Jones'" if you will. Being financially free isn't about driving the nicest car, or living in the biggest house, it's about making smart decisions with your income and managing yourself to be disciplined on what you spend your money on. If you are diligent with this approach it will set you on a path to financial freedom.

## *Control*

Control what you can control. We can't control time but we can control ourselves and what we choose to do with our time. The key to managing ourselves is invoking discipline into our choices. There are 24 hours in a day and we have a chance every single moment of NOW to make a choice to change our lives for the better. What do you choose today? What do you choose in this precious moment of NOW? What direction do you want your life to go? It's up to you... after all lack of direction, not lack of time, is the problem. We all have twenty-four hour days...

# *What Can I Do NOW?*

**I – Working Backwards -**

On a sheet of paper write down 3-5 goals that you want to achieve within the next 6-12 months. Write them out as if you have already achieved them. For instance; I have increased my annual income by 50%. NOW starting with that premise. Write down all the things you would have to do in order to bring that into your current reality. What would you have to do on a Monthly basis, weekly basis, and daily basis? This is an excellent exercise on writing precise effective goals that force you to be disciplined and concentrate on the things you can control right NOW...

**II – The Control Room Exercise -**

View the list of all the things you can control below. Notice that none of them are outside of yourself. Ask yourself this question. How can I use the things I can control to lead a happy and healthy life? Write your answers down and keep them somewhere where you can reference them when you are dealing with a troubling time in your life.

**Things you can control -**

1) **My Attitude/ My Feelings** (How I choose to feel about something)

2) **My Breath (**Focused breathing can calm and sooth the soul)

3) **My Self-talk** (What I say about myself to myself)

4) **My Actions/ and Reactions** (It's not what happens, it's how I choose to react to what happens)

5) **My Gratitude** (Counting my blessings and not my problems)

6) **My Body Language** (Smile it's good for the soul :)

# VI – Yesterday you said tomorrow

"The Time is Always NOW" - TY

Back in 2007 I was in a sales meeting for a company that I used to work for. The VP of Sales was informing us of all the great new things going on in the company and I was halfway tuned in and probably half way tuned out. I had been in these types of meetings so many times before. Then he said something that really caught my attention. He said "Today's paper is yesterday's news." Think about that for a second. The paper is so far behind. Yesterday I came home and found a Yellow book sitting on my front porch. I literally looked at it and thought for a second… "What am I supposed to do with that?" I mean by the time I look in the book to use it the addresses and phone numbers would probably be wrong. I recall being at my Mother's house a couple of years ago with both of my kids and I remember we were trying to look something up and for some reason couldn't find it online. My Mother was adamant that we look it up in the phonebook and she went on to tell my kids how important it was to be able to use the phone book. I allowed her to teach them the lesson however I did interject to explain to her that the information online is way more dependable than the information in that book. The book was created a year ago and cannot be updated until the next printing. Information online can be updated in real time, so it's better to use the information you receive online. My daughter and I were driving to a new Unity

Center for me to speak just last week. And I, being the old school guy that I am printed the directions out on paper. As soon as Yaniece saw that she asked me why didn't I just send the directions to my phone and do it that way. I told her I thought I did send it to my phone but I still wanted that paper in my hand. So we used the paper directions and wouldn't you know once we got close to our destination one of the streets on my printed directions wasn't showing up. It just wasn't there. So we were kind of loss. You see, my printed directions didn't have today's information; they had yesterday's information. We needed the information from right NOW to reach our destination. Of course Yaniece pulled out her phone and we used the navigation to get us to our destination. Yes, thank God for the beauty of technology. Information at your fingertips. It's a sign of the Information Age...

## Industrial age vs Information Age

Back in the Industrial Age which started in the late 1800's we would get all of our information from the newspaper. There was one source for information. One source to inform the masses. Of course the paper can only be printed after something happens so if something happens today you would see it in tomorrow's paper. So if you were sitting down reading your paper in 1892 you were reading today's paper but you were getting yesterday's news. This is still true to this day and this is why the paper industry is on such a steep decline. Why would anyone wait until tomorrow to get today's news? Or maybe a better way to put it... Why put off for tomorrow what you can do today? Do it NOW.

We have reached the information Age NOW. The Information Age started roughly around 1989 when the internet was created. NOW we get our news literally as it happens and we have an unlimited amount of sources to gather that news from. Most people get their news from the internet not the newspaper or the daily 6pm newscast. We have access to all of our information NOW. We don't have to wait for someone to tell us what is going on in the world. We don't have to wait to gather information that we need. We can simply search the internet and find out what is going on in the world right NOW. We can search the internet and get the information we need right NOW. So why wait? How many times have you put off for tomorrow something you could do today? Did you ever get it done? Chances are you didn't. Nothing can ever be done tomorrow. Some look at the quote from above (The Time is Always NOW) as a cliché. You know, it sounds cool to say it but it really doesn't mean anything in the "real world." I beg to differ. Life can only be experienced in the present moment. You can dream about the future but you can only do it in the present moment. You can reminisce about the past but you can only do it in the present moment. When you got up this morning it was NOW; when you rode a bike for the first time it was NOW; when you were born it was NOW. There is power that lies in the realization of this eternal truth. This is what I've come to share with you.

## There is Power in the present moment

I was a college freshman at 17 years old back in 1989. I was on a full basketball scholarship at Hillsborough Community College. I loved hanging out with the team and creating these new friendships as I started my adult life. When we started the year I befriended four guys on the team and they were all 21 years old or older. Quickly we began to do what many college students did. We partied a lot and did a lot of drinking. It wasn't long before I began to make the connection that the only way to have a good time was to drink alcohol. I mean isn't that what everybody does? At least that's the way I saw it. NOW keep in mind I'm just 17 years old at the time and still living at home. One night we were out partying like we always did after a game (sometimes before a game but I won't go there NOW) and I was too inebriated to drive myself back home to my parent's house. So the guys decided to pack me in the car and drive me home. They pulled up to my parent's house, dragged me out of the car (because I couldn't walk) and leaned me up against the door; then they rang the doorbell and drove off! Needless to say my parents weren't very happy with me the next day. Of course I had my excuses though. It wasn't my fault, it was my friend's fault for leaving me at the door like that. My Mom didn't want to hear it. The next morning she told me I had to move out. Well I did just that, the only problem was guess who I moved in with? You got it. I moved in with guys from the team. So we continued our partying ways. Needless to say we didn't win too many basketball games that year. So I graduated from HCC and went on to a full scholarship at Mercer University. Yes I was pretty good at basketball back then. The pattern continued though with my new teammates at Mercer. A lot of parties and a lot of drinking. By the time I left Mercer in 1995 I was a full-fledged functioning alcoholic.

1995 - When I returned to Tampa I just traded my basketball buddies in for my work buddies and the college parties became happy hour every Friday night. From 1995 until 2000 I continued with my addiction. There were so many nights where I would grab my keys and drive home at 2am in the morning after a long night of drinking. One night was different though...

### *The Accident*

*Summer 2000 - My coworkers and I hit up the local bar after work for Happy Hour just like any other night. I grabbed my keys and headed home around 2am. I hopped in my 1995 Plymouth Acclaim and headed down 275 North on my way home. As I was driving at about 65 mph I slowly began to drift off and fall asleep. All I remember after that was a loud bang and waking up to smoke* everywhere and people standing around. I had fell asleep at the wheel on the interstate and run off the road head on into the median. The people that were standing around were the people in the cars that were behind me. Later they told me they watched my car just drift off the road in horror. The state trooper told me that if I didn't have my seatbelt on that night I would have gone right through the windshield and most likely died. Of course I had my excuses. It wasn't my fault. It was my coworkers fault for letting me drive home. I escaped with minimal injuries so even after this serious accident I continued on with the same behavior.

2001 – Since I wasn't playing basketball anymore I took up running a little more seriously to stay in shape and I noticed something. When I ran I had no urge to drink. When I ran I felt so good that I didn't want to ruin it by drinking. I remember watching a PBS special around that same time and this guy named Dr. Wayne Dyer was on. At the time I didn't know who he was. I knew I liked what he was saying but I couldn't quite put my finger on it. He said something that really caught my attention though on one of those specials. He said "when you feel good, you feel God." I knew that at that moment I must have been feeling the presence of God when I ran. The presence of God was flowing through me and that is why I felt so good when I ran. That is why I had no urge to drink. I tell you, that special was so good I almost bought the "Whole Enchilada" because of that one statement. If you are a Wayne Dyer fan than you know what I mean… So I loved running so much that I decided that I wanted to take it further. After a couple of 5ks and 10ks I decided I wanted to run a marathon. I put my name in the lottery for the NYC marathon for November 2003. It's a lottery system so you don't know if you're going to get picked until around May of that year. Low and behold I won the lottery! How many people can say that? I got the letter in the mail that I would be running the 2003 NYC marathon. I trained hard for 5 straight months and during that time I didn't have a sip of alcohol. I had no desire to drink. Finally the day had arrived and I found myself in NYC standing at the base of the Verrazano Bridge with 30,000 of my closest friends. And the countdown begins 5…4…3…2…1 and we're off! I ran that race with a love in my heart and a pep in my step. I was high fiving all the spectators on the sidelines (there are over a million spectators at the NYC marathon). It was an amazing experience and by no means was it easy. It was very difficult and I struggled mightily for the last 10 miles of the race but I never gave up. When I saw that finish line and knew I only had 385 more yards to go I ran as hard as I could up that hill in Central Park. When I crossed the line they put that ribbon around my neck and I was like "Yes! I've done it. NOW it's time to celebrate!" And where do you think I went? I took the A train and found the first bar I could find to get myself a drink. Five months down the drain. I went right back to my old self-defeating ways. The addiction still had its hold on me. It took me seven more years before I was able to break the chains of addiction.

## *My Epiphany Moment*

February 1st 2010 - I picked up a book by an author that I was familiar with by this time. His name was Dr. Wayne Dyer and the title of the book was "Excuses Begone!" I looked at the title and I thought to myself, I've got some excuses that need to be gone. This has got to be the book for me! I found myself sitting on the floor in my little one bedroom apartment with a quart of beer thinking to myself I have got to stop this. I have to make a change in my life. I had just read the passage in Dr. Wayne Dyer's book that states **"a dysfunctional relationship with life is nothing more than a dysfunctional relationship with the present moment. Life only gets lived in the NOW."** At that very moment I decided I was going to change my life forever. I decided I would never have another drink again and I haven't since that day over 7 years ago. This was my Epiphany! I realized at that moment that I had a dysfunctional relationship with the NOW. I realized I had the power to change my life in an instant from any negative thought or self-defeating behavior. I realized that that power dwells inside of me. The Power of NOW is the power of God that lives inside us all. It is more powerful than any drug could ever be. I was finally free… Once I figured this out my whole life changed. I became a better Father, Brother, Son, Friend, Co-worker, Runner. NOW that I have experienced this power first hand I know it is my passion and my mission here on this earth to help as many people as I can tap into the power in the eternal moment of NOW to change their lives forever. This is why I'm here.

## Physically – Spiritually – Financially

Taking care of your body is an extremely important part of self-care. After all your body is the temple of your soul. I love the quote "Take care of your body, it's the only place you have to live." Have you been putting off physical activity because you feel like you can't or you "just don't have the time?" If this is speaking to you ask yourself this question... Why do you feel like you can't insert some sort of physical activity into your daily routine? Here's the important thing to remember. It doesn't matter how small the activity may seem to you it all counts in helping keep your body in the best shape it can be in. You don't have to be a marathon runner. If you can walk for 15 minutes a day, do that. If you can ride a bike for 15-20 minutes a day, do that. If you can't walk or ride than swim. Do water walking. Silver sneakers is a great fitness program designed for people 65 and up to add physical activity into their daily routines. If they can do it what's your excuse?

Are you one of those people who say they don't have time to exercise? Remember as I discussed in Chapter V. Time management is Self-management. We make time for things that we feel are important to us. Taking care of your physical well-being should be at the top of your priorities if you want to live a long, happy and healthy life. Keep in mind it really doesn't matter what you do as long as you do something consistently. There is only one time to do it and that time is NOW. The hardest part is getting started. Once you start, you will feel better and you will know that it is worth it because exercising daily is a key component to becoming **physically** free.

James 2:14. Faith without works is dead. You have to practice your **spirituality.** You have to practice your faith and you have to do it NOW. We just dealt with two huge hurricanes in the US. One, hurricane Harvey hit Texas while hurricane Irma hit Florida about 2 weeks later. Yes, we were all praying for each other in this time of need however the most important aspect of these two natural disasters was our response after the storms had passed and we had to deal with the recovery efforts. We all came together as communities and worked to help each other. We assisted each other in any way that we could. It's easy to pray for someone from a distance but the reality is when we show our faith it makes a difference. When we practice our spirituality in action, it makes a difference. When we become the face of God to someone in need it makes a difference. This is the way to set yourself free. Find a way to serve others and put it into action. Do it, do it NOW…

Are you in control of your finances? Do you know where your money is going? It takes massive action over a prolonged period of time to experience financial freedom. Most people want to become **financially** free but they don't want to put in the time to do it. They want to experience the freedom but wish it would happen overnight. It doesn't work that way. Taking action NOW is the key. If you're not where you want to be financially start by putting money away NOW. Start by investing money NOW. Start by taking the class on real estate investing NOW. Every decision counts. Every action counts no matter how small or inconsequential you may think it is. Every time you make a new decision and move away from old money habits and adopt new ones you are building the foundation that will set you on a path to financial freedom.

## *Do it NOW*

This isn't a movie and we don't get any do overs. This is your time. What have you been procrastinating on? What are you holding back on? What dream are you still dreaming but haven't brought to fruition yet? Why haven't you started? Get started today on making your dreams come true. If you want to change your life than you have to **change** your life. It's up to you. There will never be a better time to start because after all the time is always NOW...

# *What Can I Do NOW?*

I - Read the book Excuses Begone by Dr. Wayne Dyer. This is an excellent book. If you have been giving yourself excuses on why you can't achieve something in life then this is the book for you. It changed my life and it will change yours as well.

II - Practice Present Moment Techniques

A) Practice Single Task Working – Do only one thing at a time

B) Speak the words "I Am" followed by the task you are doing. Ex- I Am brushing my teeth. I Am combing my hair

C) Breathing – meditate and concentrate on your breath

D) Yoga – Find a Yoga class and attend or just start by practicing at home

E) Journal – Make time to write on a daily basis. Allot 30 minutes to an hour every day for complete silence and put your thoughts on paper.

III - If you are 65 + join Silver sneakers at www.silversneakers.com.

## *Closing*

My friend... thank you for joining me on this journey of becoming Physically, Spiritually and Financially free. It is my intention that this book is able to touch you and inspire you to take action and start living your life to its fullest potential right NOW. They say that repetition is the Mother of skill and rehearsal is the Father of learning. I encourage you to continue to use the principles taught in each chapter. Use the exercises in the "What can I do NOW "sections to help you get to where you want to be. I truly believe that most people are waiting on "someday" or "one day" to change their life when the truth is those days will never come. This is your time. The time to change your life is NOW. The time to make a better choice is NOW. The time to start living is NOW. If you've been waiting on a sign, well here it is!

CC BY-SA 3.0 Nick Youngson

I wish you continued success on your journey. My name is TY. Remember the time is always NOW. Allow the Universe to work in your favor and be blessed...

# **References**

Dyer, Wayne W. *Excuses Begone! How to Change Lifelong, Self-Defeating Thinking Habits.* - Hay House 2009

Simmons, Gary. *The I of the Storm: Embracing Conflict, Creating Peace.* - Unity House, 2006.

Wills, Amanda, Hernandez, Sergio, Baldacci, Marlena CNN article published 2017 January 1st.

# Notes

# Notes

# Notes

# Notes

# **Notes**

# Notes

Made in the USA
Columbia, SC
07 November 2021